W9-ACR-826

C I T Y !

WASHINGTON, D.C.

BY SHIRLEY CLIMO
PHOTOGRAPHS BY GEORGE ANCONA

MACMILLAN PUBLISHING COMPANY NEW YORK

COLLIER MACMILLAN CANADA TORONTO

MAXWELL MACMILLAN INTERNATIONAL PUBLISHING GROUP
NEW YORK OXFORD SINGAPORE SYDNEY

For G.F.C.

—S.C.

For Cecilia Yung

—G.A.

The author wishes to thank Dr. Howard Gillette, Jr.,
Professor of American Studies, The George Washington University,
for his assistance in reviewing the factual content of this book.

First edition   Printed in the United States of America   10 9 8 7 6 5 4 3 2 1
The text of this book is set in 12 point ITC Century Light. The photographs were taken on 35mm Kodachrome film and reproduced from color transparencies.
Library of Congress Cataloging-in-Publication Data • Climo, Shirley. City! Washington, D.C. / by Shirley Climo; photographs by George Ancona. — 1st ed.   p.   cm. Summary: Describes the building, history, and significant sights of Washington, D.C.
ISBN 0-02-719036-6
1. Washington (D.C.)—Description—1981–   —Guide-books—Juvenile literature. 2. Washington (D.C.)—History—Juvenile literature. [1. Washington (D.C.)] I. Ancona, George. ill. II. Title. F192.3.C57 1991   917.5304′4—dc20   90-40524 CIP AC

CONTENTS

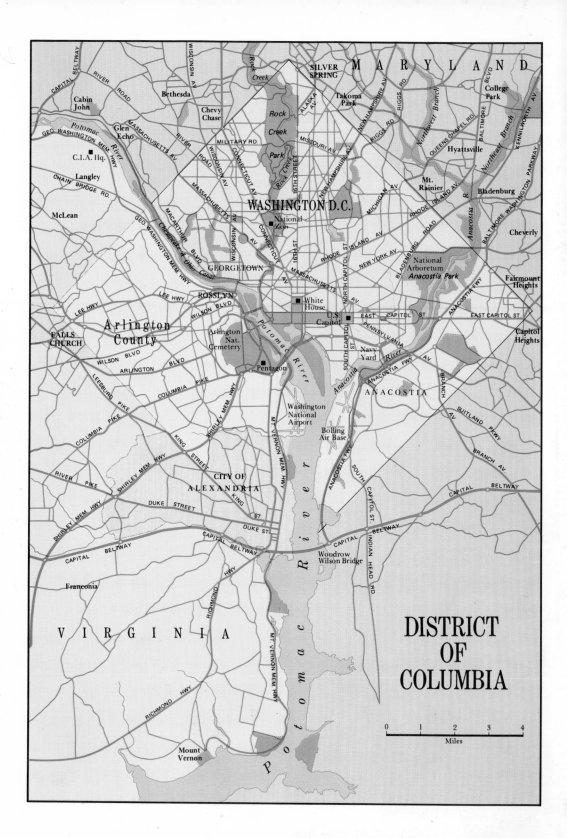

CAPITAL BELTWAY
RIVER ROAD
Bethesda
Cabin John
Chevy Chase
Glen Echo
Potomac River
GEO. WASHINGTON MEM. HWY.
C.I.A. Hq.
Langley
CHAIN BRIDGE RD.
McLean
MASSACHUSETTS AV.
RIVER ROAD
MILITARY RD.
WISCONSIN AV.
CONNECTICUT AV.
MACARTHUR BLVD.
Chesapeake & Ohio Canal
GEO. WASHINGTON MEM. HWY.
GEORGETOWN
WISCONSIN AV.
CONNECTICUT AV.
LEE HWY
ROSSLYN
WILSON BLVD
Arlington County
LEE HWY
FALLS CHURCH
WILSON BLVD
ARLINGTON BLVD
LEESBURG PIKE
COLUMBIA PIKE
COLUMBIA PIKE
RIVER PIKE
SHIRLEY MEM. HWY
KING STREET
SHIRLEY MEM. HWY
CITY OF ALEXANDRIA
KING ST.
DUKE STREET
DUKE ST.
SHIRLEY MEM. HWY
CAPITAL BELTWAY
CAPITAL BELTWAY
Franconia
RICHMOND HWY
MT. VERNON MEM. HWY
VIRGINIA
RICHMOND HWY
MT. VERNON MEM. HWY
Mount Vernon

SILVER SPRING
MARYLAND
Rock Creek
ALASKA AV.
Takoma Park
NEW HAMPSHIRE AV.
Rock Creek Park
MISSOURI AV.
16TH STREET
Rock Creek
WASHINGTON D.C.
National Zoo
RHODE ISLAND ST.
16TH ST.
MICHIGAN AV.
NEW YORK AV.
MASSACHUSETTS AV.
White House
U.S. Capitol
NORTH CAPITOL ST.
EAST CAPITOL ST.
Arlington Nat. Cemetery
Pentagon
Potomac River
SOUTH CAPITOL ST.
Navy Yard
PENNSYLVANIA AV.
Anacostia River
ANACOSTIA FWY.
ANACOSTIA
Washington National Airport
Bolling Air Base
ANACOSTIA FWY.
SOUTH CAPITOL ST.
River
Woodrow Wilson Bridge
CAPITAL BELTWAY
INDIAN HEAD RD.
Potomac River
Potomac

RIGGS RD.
Northwest Branch
QUEENS CHAPEL RD.
RIGGS RD.
Hyattsville
BALTIMORE BLVD
College Park
KENILWORTH AV.
BALTIMORE-WASHINGTON PARKWAY
Mt. Rainier
RHODE ISLAND AV.
BLADENBURG ROAD
Bladensburg
Northeast Branch
Anacostia R.
Cheverly
National Arboretum
Anacostia Park
ANACOSTIA FWY.
Fairmount Heights
EAST CAPITOL ST.
Capitol Heights
BRANCH AV.
SUITLAND PKWY.
BRANCH AV.
CAPITAL BELTWAY

0   1   2   3   4
Miles

DISTRICT
OF
COLUMBIA

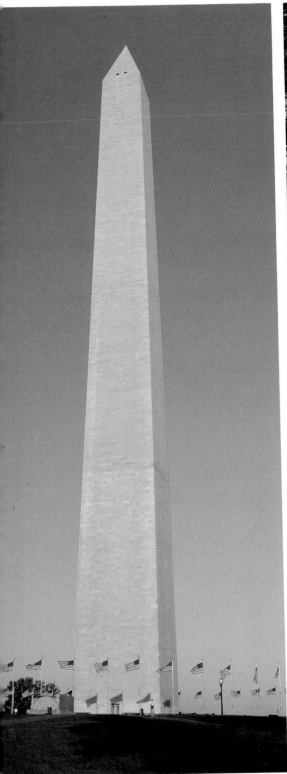

▲ A.　B.▲　C.▼

A. Fifty American flags, one for each state, circle the Washington Monument. B. The Capitol is the most important building in Washington—and the nation. C. The Lincoln Memorial honors Abraham Lincoln, our sixteenth president.

WELCOME TO WASHINGTON!

Most of America's great cities weren't planned. They just happened. A particular group of people arrived in a particular place, and then, stone by stone, street by street, year after year, a town grew.

That's not true of Washington, D.C. No band of Pilgrims sought out this site. No pioneers stumbled upon it. No missionaries founded a settlement here. No soldiers raised a fortress. Washington was built to order, and the order to build it came from the Congress of the United States. Our nation was the first to create its capital.

In 1790, members of Congress voted to set aside a tract of land along the Potomac River for the federal government. They called this territory the District of Columbia in honor of Christopher Columbus, the man who discovered the Western Hemisphere. But before even a brick was laid or a roof beam raised, people began labeling the capital Washington. Embarrassed, George Washington simply called it the "Federal City." Not until after the president's death did the capital officially become Washington, D.C.

D.C. stands for the District of Columbia, and those initials are an important part of the city's address. They help to avoid confusion with the state of Washington and with the dozens of cities across the country that are also namesakes of our first president.

Our capital city was built to be the showplace of the nation. Stately buildings are set among green parklands and along broad avenues, but it is the Washington Monument that catches every eye. This four-sided pillar soars up for over 555 feet. It's the tallest masonry structure on earth, and the only skyscraper in Washington. No high-rise buildings are allowed to spoil the scene within the city limits.

By day, sunlight polishes the white dome of the Capitol. At night, floodlights gild the bronze statue *Freedom* on top of the dome. This is the city's most imitated building. Half the capitols of our fifty states are close copies of it.

Although *capital* and *capitol* sound the same, they're spelled differently. The city where a seat of government is located ends with *al*. The building where lawmakers meet ends with *ol*. To distinguish it from others, the nation's Capitol, the house where Congress considers national matters, is written with yet another kind of capital—a capital *C*!

Other famous Washington landmarks should look as familiar as old friends. Is there a penny in your pocket? On one side of a one-cent coin is a portrait of Abraham Lincoln. Flip it over and you'll see the Lincoln Memorial. A five-dollar bill also shows the Lincoln Memorial on its reverse side, and a likeness of the Treasury Building is on the back of a ten-dollar bill. If you're lucky enough to have a twenty-dollar bill, then you have a picture of the White House, too.

A. ▲ B. ▼

OPPOSITE PAGE: A. Demonstrators gather in Lafayette Park across from the White House. B. Each spring, a million visitors come to the capital for the Cherry Blossom Festival.

THIS PAGE: A. The huge doors leading into the Capitol tell the story of Christopher Columbus. B. The Mall is everyone's park.

A. ▲ B. ▼

Inside these magnificent buildings, Washington is minding its business. That business is running the government of the United States, and it's the biggest business in the world.

Three branches of state oversee our country's affairs: the president and his administration, members of Congress and their aides, the Supreme Court justices and their staff. But our founding fathers never guessed how the government would grow. When the capital moved from Philadelphia to Washington in 1800, there were just 126 clerks on the payroll. Now, about four hundred thousand people in the Washington area work for the federal government.

Tourism is Washington's second-largest business. Twenty million sightseers crowd into the capital each year. But for the past two hundred years, visitors to this city have complained about the climate. Mark Twain, author of *Huckleberry Finn*, advised Washington tourists to bring "an overcoat, a fan, and an umbrella."

If you visit in the winter, you'll certainly need an overcoat, for the thermometer can suddenly plunge below freezing. Our second president, John Adams, and his wife, Abigail, first arrived at the White House on a frosty November afternoon. Although the president's mansion had thirteen fireplaces, wood to burn in them was scarce. Some rooms were so chilly that conversations could be seen as well as heard.

On a summer day, the temperature can nudge one hundred degrees Fahrenheit, so don't forget your fan. Washington is humid as well as hot, for it lies between two rivers, the Potomac and the Anacostia. It's claimed that the first foreign ambassadors to the capital asked for hardship pay for enduring the sticky summers. Now you can beat the heat inside an air-conditioned building or cool off with an ice-cream cone from a sidewalk vendor. Ice cream has been in style in Washington since Dolley Madison, wife of our fourth president, served it to guests in the White House.

Autumn days are bright and crisp, and the city hums with busyness. Members of Congress return from summer vacations, the Supreme Court sits in session, and the squirrels, year-round Washington residents, stop begging popcorn from tourists long enough to bury acorns in the parks.

Washington is at its most inviting in the spring. In April, cherry trees bloom beside the Tidal Basin. Blossoms, like drifts of pink snowflakes, swirl on the bare branches. In 1912, the city of Tokyo sent three thousand cherry trees to our capital as a present. Helen Taft, wife of President William Howard Taft, planted the first of the small saplings.

In springtime, Washington weather suggests picnics on the Mall or in another park. But bring along an umbrella, just the same.

In any season, welcome to Washington. Because the District of Columbia does not belong to any one state, it belongs to all of the people in all the fifty states. You are one of this city's two hundred forty million landlords. Wherever you live in America, this is your hometown.

A.▲ B.▼ C.▼

A. Uncle Beazley, a fiberglass *Triceratops*, welcomes today's visitors to the National Museum of Natural History. B. Inside the museum are bones from prehistoric visitors. C. An Indian greets Pilgrims in this scene on the frieze, or band, that decorates the Capitol rotunda.

T W O

BEGINNINGS

Washington's first visitor may have been an eighty-foot *Brachiosaurus*. One hundred fifty million years ago, dinosaurs wallowed in the cypress swamp that underlies much of our present-day capital.

As workers dig foundations for buildings, they occasionally unearth remains of prehistoric creatures. Now some of these fossils from Washington's past have found permanent lodging in the National Museum of Natural History. A three-horned *Triceratops*, molded from fiberglass, greets you outside the museum, while, inside, skeletons of real dinosaurs stretch their bony necks high overhead.

Long after the last of these giant reptiles had disappeared, the first people arrived on the banks of the Potomac River. Different groups of Native Americans fished the river and hunted its shores for many thousands of years before Columbus crossed the Atlantic Ocean. The round-domed dwellings of a village named Tohoga once clustered where the brick houses of Washington's Georgetown section now stand. At the foot of a hill, Powhatan Indians built a council house to talk over tribal matters. Today, the Capitol Building stands at the top of that same hill.

In 1608, Captain John Smith, with a company of "seven soldiers and seven gentlemen," set sail in an open barge from Jamestown, Virginia. He mapped the Potomac River and swapped tools and trinkets with Indians for food and furs. Others followed Captain Smith, and soon the farms of Scottish and English settlers took over the Indian hunting grounds.

Diseases such as smallpox came with the newcomers, and the number of Native Americans dwindled. By 1675, they had vanished, like the dinosaurs before them. But the Indians left far more than bones behind. As well as introducing us to corn and potatoes, they gave us new words like *opposum, wigwam, skunk,* and *squash.* They also named the Potomac River, which means "trading place" in the Algonquin tongue. (European settlers, unsure of the spelling, wrote *Potomac* in seventeen different ways!)

Two hundred years ago, what is now the District of Columbia was muddy marshland and meadows. But President George Washington saw beyond the swamps and fields and imagined the nation's capital growing here instead. The new republic desperately needed a permanent place for its government, for, by 1790, the country already had had eight temporary capitals.

Northern Congressmen called for a site in the north. Southern Congressmen insisted on a southern location.

Then Thomas Jefferson, who was secretary of state, invited Alexander Hamilton, who was secretary of the treasury, to dinner. Jefferson was from Virginia and favored the southern point of view. Hamilton was from New York and represented the northern position. But by the time they had finished dessert, the two men had worked out a solution. The nation would create a separate territory for the capital, supervised by commissioners appointed by Congress. Washington was made to order from a compromise reached at a dinner table.

Congress asked George Washington to select the actual site on the "bank of the Potowmac River." President Washington rode on horseback along the Potomac for eighty miles and finally decided on a one-hundred-square-mile tract, divided down the middle by the river. A smaller river, the Anacostia, and a large stream, Rock Creek, also flowed through the chosen territory. The location was central to the thirteen states, for it lay midway between two important cities: Boston to the north and Charleston to the south.

For this new District of Columbia, the state of Maryland gave up 69.25 square miles, and Virginia 30.75 square miles. Two existing towns were included within the boundaries— Alexandria in Virginia and George Town (now Georgetown) in Maryland. George Town wasn't named for George Washington, but for George II, king of England.

Washington chose a young Frenchman, Pierre Charles L'Enfant, to draw up the plans for the federal capital. L'Enfant had come to this country to fight in the American Revolution and served with Washington at Valley Forge.

A. On the rotunda frieze, the Indian princess Pocahontas saves the life of English explorer John Smith.
B. A nineteen and a half-foot statue of Thomas Jefferson, our third president, dominates the Jefferson Memorial.
C. The Jefferson Memorial, overlooking the Tidal Basin, resembles Monticello, Jefferson's own home.

A. ▲

B. ▲ C. ▼

A. ▲   B. ▼   C. ▼

A. The Lincoln Memorial is seen from the grave site of our thirty-fifth president, John F. Kennedy. B. Once a separate city, Georgetown is the oldest section of Washington, D.C. C. The view from Pierre L'Enfant's grave in Arlington National Cemetery is of the capital that he designed.

Besides being a soldier, Major L'Enfant was an architect and an engineer. He dreamed of building a city "magnificent enough to grace a great nation." He laid out the capital in the shape of a wheel, with avenues as its spokes and the "Federal House"—the Capitol—as its hub. East–west streets were given the letters of the alphabet, north–south streets were numbered, and the broad avenues were named for the states. The most important avenue, where the president's house would stand, was called Pennsylvania.

Major L'Enfant's ideas were grand, too grand for folks with simpler tastes and tighter fists. Many called him "that spendthrift Frenchman." L'Enfant designed avenues a full 160 feet wide, and if a tree or even a house stood in the way of his plan, he ordered it pulled down. The three commissioners for the District of Columbia asked L'Enfant to make changes, but he angrily refused. The commisioners, equally angry, persuaded President Washington to fire L'Enfant. Insulted, the French major stormed from the city, taking his detailed drawings for the capital with him.

Now the task of laying out the city fell to L'Enfant's assistant, Andrew Ellicott. Working from notes made by L'Enfant and by his surveyor, a free African American mathematician named Benjamin Banneker, Ellicott drew up the first official map of the city. At last, with President Washington's dream transferred to paper, the building of the nation's capital could begin.

THREE

◀———————————▶

WINNERS
AND LOSERS

Washington got off to a prize-winning start. A nationwide contest was announced to find the best design for the president's house. Although Thomas Jefferson submitted a sketch (signed with the initials A.Z. to hide his identity), the winner was an architect named James Hoban. Hoban had been born in Ireland, and his drawing for our nation's number-one home resembled the grand Irish manor houses he'd admired as a boy. This "President's Palace" is the oldest public building in Washington. The cornerstone, the first foundation block, was laid on October 12, 1792, three hundred years after Columbus discovered America.

President John Adams and his wife were the first First Family to live in the president's house. Although Abigail Adams called it a "great castle," the house was not yet finished. The roof leaked, walls lacked plaster, and there was no drying yard for the laundry. Mrs. Adams had the wash hung to dry in the huge reception hall at the east end. The sheets on the line billowed like sails in that drafty room.

Still, on November 2, 1800, the president wrote:

I pray Heaven to Bestow the Best of Blessings on this House and all that shall hereafter Inhabit it. May none but Honest and Wise Men ever rule under this Roof.

One hundred thirty-five years later, President Franklin D. Roosevelt had those words carved into the marble mantel of the State Dining Room.

For the site of the nation's Capitol, L'Enfant had chosen Jenkins Hill. He referred to this height, which rises eighty-eight feet above the banks of the Potomac River, as a "pedestal waiting for a monument." The monument was to be the "Congress House," and newspapers around the country advertised another competition for *its* design. This time the winner of the five-hundred-dollar prize was a physician, Dr. William Thornton. His drawing featured two identical wings, one for the Senate and one for the House of Representatives, joined by a round, domed center room called a *rotunda*.

On September 18, 1793, bands played while George Washington himself put down the Capitol's cornerstone, cementing it with a silver trowel. A finger-licking celebration ended the ceremony. A five-hundred-pound ox had been roasted, and everyone sat down to a barbecue.

OPPOSITE PAGE: George Washington was the only president who did not live in the White House.

THIS PAGE: Both the United States Senate and the House of Representatives meet in the Capitol.

Construction of the Capitol dragged. There were never enough men, money, or materials to do the job. In 1800, the year Congress had set for the move to Washington, only the north wing was ready. Without the other wing and the rotunda, the building looked like a giant packing box. That's what it turned out to be, for the Senate, the House of Representatives, the circuit court, the Supreme Court, and the Library of Congress all had to squeeze within its walls. On hot summer days the building got so stuffy it was nicknamed "The Oven." Senators and representatives fared no better in their lodgings. They slept two to a bed in taverns and boardinghouses, and only the Speaker of the House had a mattress to himself.

Ordinary people added to the overcrowding on Capitol Hill. Eating and gossiping were the two most popular pastimes in Washington, and the best place to do both was in the Capitol building. When Congress was in session, people even picnicked in the galleries. Sometimes snacks were tied to long poles and sent up to onlookers from the floor of the House.

Construction continued in the capital. Within a few years, buildings for the Treasury, State, War, and Navy departments, as well as the Patent and Post offices, joined official Washington. But unofficial Washington still looked like a country village. Only a few hundred houses, mostly wood, were scattered along the unpaved streets. In dry weather, horses kicked up whirlwinds of dust, and after a rain the carriage ruts ran with water like canals. At any time, cows and pigs roamed freely in the roads, and corn grew on Pennsylvania Avenue.

The United States of America was expanding rapidly, both in size and in importance. By March of 1809, when James Madison was sworn in as the fourth president, the nation was on its way to becoming a world power.

Despite that, England and France, at war with each other, plagued American ships at sea. Then Britain began to *impress,* or kidnap, United States sailors from those ships. Angry Americans demanded that their country's honor be defended. In June of 1812, Congress declared war on England. History books in the United States call this conflict the War of 1812.

Most of the battles in the war were naval clashes. Then American troops burned the city of York, now Toronto, in Canada. England was determined to even the score. On August 24, 1814, a British force of forty-five hundred men marched upon Washington. The defending American militia, ill-equipped and ill-trained, scattered before the attackers. Filling baskets with important papers, and wagons with whatever else they could lay hold of, government officials fled. Before she abandoned the White House, Dolley Madison, the president's wife, ordered Gilbert Stuart's portrait of George Washington to be broken from its frame and carried from the city to safety.

English Rear Admiral Sir George Cockburn stormed into the deserted House of Representatives. "Shall this harbor of Yankee democracy be burned?" he asked.

"Aye! Aye!" shouted his men.

They piled up the desks and chairs and kindled a huge bonfire. Just twenty-one years after President Washington had laid the cornerstone, the Capitol burned to the ground.

The White House, too, with its treasures and fine furnishings, was set on fire. A heavy rainstorm in the night put out the flames, but the building was gutted.

The next morning, the British torched the Treasury, State, and Navy buildings, the newspaper office, and many private homes. Then suddenly that afternoon, gale-force winds swept in, strong enough to tip cannons from their mounts. The English troops withdrew, but they left a burned-out, smokey shambles behind them. Although the United States would win the war, Washington had lost the day.

A. ▲ B. ▼   C. ▼   D. ▼

A. To paint the high dome of the rotunda, artist Constantino Brumidi lay on his back on a scaffold. B. This painting of George Washington by Gilbert Stuart joins a dozen other likenesses of the first president in the National Portrait Gallery. C. The National Portrait Gallery is housed in the old U.S. Patent Office, Washington's third oldest building. D. An early model of a washing machine is a reminder that this building was originally the Patent Office.

FOUR

←————————————→

SYMBOLS FOR
AMERICA

The burning of Washington wasn't the end of the city. Instead, the fire sparked a new beginning. At first, Congress considered moving the capital. Then the lawmakers realized that the buildings in Washington had become important symbols for the United States. They voted to rebuild.

Because its sandstone exterior was light in color, the president's home had sometimes been called the White House. But after that August day in 1814, only a blackened, burned-out shell remained. James Hoban, the architect, dug out his original plans, and construction began again. Three years later, when our fifth president, James Monroe, moved in, coats of glossy white paint concealed the scorched stone. Now it was truly the White House. Theodore Roosevelt made that name official in 1901 when he had it printed on his presidential stationery.

George Washington was the only president who never lived in the White House. He died in 1799, before it was first completed. The White House has been home to forty presidents since, but it has been owned by none. Franklin D. Roosevelt said, "I never forget that the house I live in belongs to all the people."

Every president has left behind some reminder of his stay. Andrew Jackson piped in running water, and Millard Fillmore bought the first cookstove. Before that, even state dinners were cooked in an open fireplace. James Polk installed gaslights, and Benjamin Harrison brought in electricity. William Howard Taft commissioned a bathtub big enough for four men, and President Franklin D. Roosevelt put in a swimming pool. Other presidents added everything from elevators to executive offices. The old structure could not support so many improvements, and, by 1948, the White House was in danger of collapsing. President Harry S Truman called for a complete reconstruction, a job that took four years.

The restored White House that you visit today has twenty baths and one hundred thirty-two rooms, but only five are open to the public. Jacqueline Kennedy, wife of President John F. Kennedy, furnished these to look as they did in the last century. You would almost expect Dolley Madison to greet you at the door.

Out of sight in the White House are the first family's private quarters; the president's oval office; staff rooms; kitchens and supply rooms; a dentist's office; a medical clinic; rooms for a barber and a florist; a movie theater; carpentry, paint, and upholstery shops; and an electrical center. The White House is a city in itself.

Five years after the British destroyed the original building, Congress moved into a new Capitol. As Dr. William

Thornton had planned, a rotunda connected the two large wings. Each congressman had a private lobby where visitors and those seeking favors might wait to talk with him. Today we call anyone who comes to the Capitol in hopes of influencing a vote or decision a *lobbyist.*

In 1829, Daniel Webster, one of the country's most famous statesmen, appointed a boy to run errands in the Senate. That nine-year-old was the first recorded Senate *page,* a name taken from the middle ages, when page boys served the knights. Today, about one hundred girls and boys from fourteen to eighteen years of age serve in Congress. They receive generous allowances and free housing, but they must get up very early in the morning to attend high-school classes before their congressional duties begin. Anybody may apply to be a page. Someday *you* might be picked for the privilege.

As more states joined the Union, more senators and more representatives joined those already in Washington. In 1851, an overcrowded Congress voted to expand the Capitol Building. Ten years later, when Abraham Lincoln became president, the new cast-iron dome still was not finished. Lincoln ordered the work to continue, declaring, "If the people see the Capitol going on, it is a sign we intend the nation shall go on."

The sculpture *Freedom,* which crowns the nine-million-pound dome, was finally swung into place on December 2, 1863. Because the statue is of a woman wearing a feathered helmet, some tourists confuse her with the Indian princess Pocahontas. The statue is so often struck by lightning that *Freedom* wears a band of lightning rods as well.

In 1959, the Capitol was again enlarged. President Dwight D. Eisenhower laid the new cornerstone with the same silver trowel that George Washington used to mortar the original. Now the Capitol has 540 rooms, including restaurants and kitchens, post offices, a prayer room, and a barbershop. Both the Senate and the House of Representatives have subways running between their six office buildings on Capitol Hill and the Capitol itself. But you don't have to be a member of Congress to ride this underground trolley. Hop aboard. It's fun—and it's free.

The halls where the senators and the representatives meet are called *chambers*. Each house has always kept its own quarters in order, but in the early days neither paid attention to the Rotunda. Vendors set up stalls, hawking everything from melons to mousetraps. Orange peels and other rubbish littered the floors. In 1864, congressmen cleaned house and turned the merchants out. They also invited all the states to send statues of heroes for display in the old House chamber. Called Statuary Hall, it's also known by its nickname, Whispering Hall. The softest murmur carries across the room, so be careful not to whisper any secrets here!

Each session of Congress has a number. In 1800, the Sixth Congress became the first to assemble in the new

A. This congressional page, on duty in Washington, comes from the state of New Mexico.
B. Subway cars carry members of Congress from their office buildings to the Capitol.
C. In Statuary Hall, statues of famous Americans stare back at visitors.

A. ▲ B. ▲ C. ▼

capital. The Congress meeting in 1991 is the One Hundred Second. When the House is in session, our nation's flag flies over the south wing of the Capitol. And when the Senate meets, the flag flies over the north wing. (Often the Senate and the House are in session at the same time, and two flags are flying.) If Congress works at night, the fifty-foot lantern on top of the Capitol dome is lighted. In years past, that beacon called members of Congress from hotels and houses all over the city.

There are one hundred senators, two from each of the fifty states. The vice president of the United States presides over the Senate. Democrats sit to his right, Republicans sit to his left, and all seats are assigned. Daniel Webster carved his name inside his desk drawer, and you can still read it clearly more that 150 years later.

Each state elects members to the House of Representatives according to its population, so the states with the greatest number of residents have the greatest number of representatives. However, by law, the House cannot have more than 435 members. The Speaker of the House is the leader and is selected by the political party that has elected the most members to the House. Democrats sit to his right and Republicans to his left, but they may choose their own seats. Once, they even chose to replace their chairs with soft couches!

Members of Congress are lawmakers, and they live up to that name. Although they introduce thousands of proposed laws each year, only about one in every twenty-five reaches the president's desk to be signed into law. If the president does not like the bill, he cancels it with a *veto*. To override, or set aside, a presidential veto, senators and representatives vote again. If two-thirds of each branch still favor the bill, it becomes a law in spite of the president.

For almost a century, when a senator or representative needed information, he sent a page skipping down a hall in the Capitol Building to fetch a book from the Library of Congress. When the Capitol burned in 1814, all the books went up in flames, as well. To begin anew, Congress purchased Thomas Jefferson's personal library. Some of his six thousand volumes are still on the shelves of the Library of Congress today.

Now the library is housed in three magnificent buildings. Each working day, the staff answers more than seventeen hundred queries from senators and representatives. If information is needed during a floor debate, it can be sent to the Capitol through an underground tube, like a toy subway.

Besides members of Congress, the library serves many others. Scholars from every nation study there. As the world's largest library, it now has 535 miles of bookshelves!

Each year, the library receives two copies of every book published in the United States, including this one. If you flip back to the beginning, you will find the Library of Congress cataloging information.

There are more than books in the library's collection.

Its treasures include everything from the first draft of the Declaration of Independence, handwritten by Thomas Jefferson, to an exhibit of Barbie and Ken dolls. There are eighty-three million different items, and every minute there are ten new additions! You could spend a couple of centuries in the Library of Congress and still not see it all.

The library has a distinguished next-door neighbor on Capitol Hill: the Supreme Court. The building looks like a pillared temple and is made of rosy Vermont marble. It's so dazzling that even on a cloudy day you have to squint to read the words above the great bronze doors, "Equal Justice under Law."

Although L'Enfant's plans called for a "House of Justice" to be built as soon as possible, the nation's highest court didn't have a home of its own for 147 years. It heard cases in boardinghouses, in a tavern, and in seven different rooms in the Capitol.

The Supreme Court is made up of nine judges, or *jus-*

tices. They determine if decisions made by lower courts are constitutional. The justices also rule whether or not acts of Congress and actions of the president keep faith with the Constitution. No other country in the world has such as powerful court.

Justices are appointed for life. When there's a vacancy on the Court, the president nominates a new judge, but the Senate must approve the choice. In 1981, President Ronald Reagan appointed Sandra Day O'Connor, the first woman to sit on the Supreme Court.

When the justices finally moved into their own building in 1935, they refused the new, carved chairs in favor of their old comfortable chairs. Each judge still personally selects his or her own seat. When a judge retires, the chair goes, too. The other justices present it as a farewell gift.

The Capitol, the White House, and the Supreme Court are more than symbols. They not only tell the nation's history, they also show us history in the making.

FIVE

TIMES OF
TROUBLE

Washington grew fastest in times of trouble. Unless things changed for the worse in the capital, nothing changed for the better, either. In the first half of the nineteenth century, the District of Columbia hardly grew at all. Although it was often crowded with visitors, only about five hundred people a year came to stay. By 1840, the population of New York City was already ten times larger than Washington's. Still, being smaller had one big advantage. For the city's first decade, only a single policeman was needed to keep the peace.

President Washington had hoped that the capital would be a major port. But large sailing ships found it difficult to navigate the Potomac, and the Chesapeake & Ohio Canal, intended to make trade with the west easier, only reached as far as Maryland.

In Georgetown, on the Fourth of July in 1828, President John Quincy Adams dug the first shovelful of dirt to begin the canal. In Baltimore, on that same holiday, the first spike was driven to begin the Baltimore and Ohio Railroad. Since both canal and railroad followed almost the same route, the two were rivals. When work on the railroad was completed first, Washington fell behind in the race to tap the rich resources of the west and never became a vital trading center.

In 1846, members of Congress approved Virginia's request for the return of the territory that state had given for the capital city. Although the Washington metropolitan area sprawls well into Virginia today, officially the District of Columbia covers only sixty-nine square miles.

The city's early lack of growth was due in part to lack of money. Without a crisis, Congress was slow to open the public purse. The Treasury Building, destroyed in 1814, wasn't replaced until 1835. Congressmen argued about both the cost and the location. Legend says that President Andrew Jackson, sick of the squabbling, struck his cane on the ground and shouted, "Put it here!" Whether or not that story is true, the plot chosen for Washington's third-oldest building was not a very good one. The Treasury spoils the view from the White House to the Capitol.

Pierre L'Enfant had selected a site for a statue of George Washington on horseback. Although Congress was pleased with the idea, more than thirty years passed before it voted to pay a sculptor. When the statue was unveiled, horrified members of Congress saw the country's first president seated not on a horse but in a chair, draped in a robe and bare chested. The statue is now in the National Museum of American History.

A. ▲ B. ▼

C. ▼

A. The statue of General Andrew Jackson, the seventh president, stands across the street from the White House. B. This statue of George Washington wears only a Roman toga. C. Camels parade at the National Zoological Park.

A. "The Castle," first home for the nation's treasures, is now the information center for the Smithsonian Institution. B. At the Arts and Industries Building, old tools, machines, and Samuel F. B. Morse's first telegraph are on exhibit. C. Visitors are "transported" by early steam engines at the National Museum of American History. D. The original "Star-Spangled Banner," proudly hailed by Francis Scott Key in our national anthem, is displayed hourly at the National Museum of American History.

◄ A.   B. ▼

C. ▼   D. ▼

In 1848, ground was broken for an entirely different kind of memorial—the Washington Monument. Unfortunately, construction funds ran out when the obelisk was only 160 feet tall. Mark Twain said it looked like "a factory chimney with the top broken off."

On the country's one hundredth birthday in 1876, Congress set aside the money to finish the job. Nine years later, on George Washington's birthday, the monument was dedicated. When a steam elevator was installed, only men could use it. Women and children weren't allowed to ride in such a risky device, so they had to climb the 898 steps to the top.

In 1835, Congress was given a gift—and a riddle. A wealthy Englishman named James Smithson had willed his money to the United States, a country he had never even seen. He left half a million dollars in gold for the establishment of the "Smithsonian Institution . . . to increase . . . knowledge among men."

Congress puzzled over how to spend this unexpected— and to some, unwanted—present. Almost twenty years passed before a red sandstone building was completed. Looking like a storybook castle, this was the first of the Smithsonian museums. Now fourteen museums in Washington, the National Zoo, and the Cooper-Hewitt Museum in New York City are included in the Smithsonian Institution. The fifteenth, the National Museum of the American Indian, is scheduled to open in 1998. Together, these museums are caretakers for the largest and most curious collection of things—historical, scientific, natural, and artistic—in the world. No wonder the Smithsonian Institution is nicknamed "Uncle Sam's attic"!

Since the first timbers of the White House were raised, African Americans have had a hand in constructing the nation's capital. Although Washington began as a slave-holding city, it has long offered opportunities to African Americans, too. As early as 1807, free blacks could attend school in the District of Columbia. The city was also an important station in the Underground Railroad, the organization that helped escaping slaves reach safety. On the eve of the Civil War, less than a quarter of the eleven thousand African Americans in Washington, D.C., were slaves.

For many years, members of Congress from the north and from the south had quarreled about politics and policies. The election of Abraham Lincoln, a northerner, as president, sparked a rebellion by southern states. The War Between the States lasted four terrible years, from 1861 until 1865. Although Washington itself was not damaged, it was in the center of the conflict. Forts for the defense of the capital surrounded the city, and every hill bristled with guns.

Soldiers camped in the ballroom of the White House. The basement of the Capitol became an army bakery, and a slaughterhouse was set up next to the unfinished Washington Monument. City churches were converted to hospitals. Clara Barton, the nurse who started the American

A. The Grant Memorial at the foot of Capitol Hill captures the action and the agony of the Civil War. B. Hostesses wear Civil War dress to guide visitors through the Robert E. Lee Memorial. C. Arlington House, home of Robert E. Lee, is maintained as a memorial to the Confederate general.

A. The equestrian bronze of General Ulysses S. Grant is the second-largest statue in the world. B. President Abraham Lincoln was fatally wounded while attending a play at Ford's Theatre. C. The expressive face and hands of Abraham Lincoln make the statue in the Lincoln Memorial world famous. D. President Lincoln died in the Petersen House, across the street from Ford's Theatre.

A. ▼   B. ▼

C. ▼

D. ▼

Red Cross, and Louisa May Alcott, the author of *Little Women*, were among those who came to the capital to care for the wounded. The poet Walt Whitman also performed nursing duties.

During the Civil War, the total population of Washington doubled from sixty thousand to one hundred twenty thousand. After President Lincoln's Emancipation Proclamation, thousands of former slaves poured into the city. Soon the city was growing not by five hundred people a year but by five hundred a day! There weren't enough houses, and black people in particular were crammed into shacks hastily built by greedy contractors. Water was in short supply, ditches ran with open sewage, and disease swept the city. President Lincoln's own son Willie was one of the many people who died of typhoid fever.

The capital was such a shambles after the war that Congress reorganized the local government. In 1871, the District of Columbia became a territory with a governor appointed by the president and an assembly elected by the people.

Washington began to rebuild and renew. Sewers were installed, sidewalks were laid, street lamps lit, and eighty miles of roads were paved. Ground was broken for magnificent new buildings. The State, War and Navy Building (now the Executive Office Building) took seventeen years to build, but when it was finished it covered four and a half acres and was the largest office building in the world.

The renewal was impressive, but so was the cost. The

city could not pay the twenty two million dollar bill. In 1874, using mismanagement as an excuse, Congress again appointed three commissioners to govern the District of Columbia. Anti-black feeling was also a part of this decision. Fearful that the African American population might gain control of the nation's capital, members of Congress took away the District's self government. Washington became the only city in the United States where people could not elect their own officials.

World War I touched off another population explosion in the nation's capital. Although the fighting was in faraway Europe, the headquarters for the war effort was in Washington. Patriotic residents melted down thousands of brass spittoons for armaments, and President Woodrow Wilson grazed sheep on the White House lawn so that the gardeners could join the military. One hundred thousand people flocked to the capital to take wartime jobs. Flimsy temporary houses, called "tempos," were thrown up, and so many automobiles arrived on the scene that the Mall became a giant parking lot.

Although boom times followed wartime, the 1930s brought the Great Depression. Jobs were scarce everywhere in the United States, except in Washington. In 1932, eighty thousand World War I veterans marched to the capital, demanding the bonus money promised for their military service. When Congress refused payment, riots followed.

Action was needed to reassure an anxious nation. The

government introduced new services and agencies, and two hundred thousand more people joined the Washington work force. They came to stay, for World War II, with *its* need for manpower, soon began.

Nineteen fifty-five marked the first year that the majority of people living in the capital were African American. Today blacks make up about 70 percent of the populace, and Washington is truly an African American city. Some of the nation's wealthiest blacks live here, and so do some of the nation's poorest. What to do for those who live in poverty is one of the capital's challenging questions.

For many years Washington has lacked necessary funds for social programs, for education, even for fire and police departments. The homeless sleep in parks, and criminals roam the streets. But more money cannot cure all of Washington's problems. The capital needs strong leadership, and for that it needs strong local government, too.

In 1973, for the first time in almost a century, Congress gave Washington's citizens the right to choose a mayor and city officials. But many Washingtonians say that is not enough. They call Washington "the last colony" and demand voting representatives in Congress, too. They would like the District of Columbia to be the fifty-first state, named New Columbia. No one is sure when or if that will happen. Before it becomes a state, Washington must first resolve its problems as a city.

D. ▼

A. ▲   B. ▼

C. ▼

A. A man with his belongings takes shelter in a bus stop. B. The entrance to the Capital Children's Museum leads into a fantasy world. C. There's something for everyone along Washington's streets. D. The new building for the National Museum of African Art opened in 1987.

←——————————————→

EXPLORING WASHINGTON, D.C.

Step right into the wonderful world of Washington. Most of the capital's attractions don't cost a cent, so all you'll have to spend is the time to see them.

But your time is priceless, too. In summer, tourists swarm about the city like mosquitoes, and the most popular exhibits are always crowded. To cut down on waiting-in-line time, call or write your member of Congress before you go. He or she can arrange specific times when you can join a tour of the White House, sit in on a session of Congress, or visit places like the Federal Bureau of Investigation (FBI). The address for your representative is the United States House of Representatives, Washington, DC 20515.

Getting around isn't a problem. A subway system, the Washington Metrorail, can whisk you to many of your destinations. Entering an underground Metro station is like going into a giant beehive. The vast ceilings overhead are honeycombed and glow with a creamy yellow light.

There's also the Metrobus system, as well as small buses called Tourmobiles. For the price of one ticket, you can "Ride through History," getting off or on any of these minibuses whenever you wish.

Tops for transportation are your own two feet, for walking through Washington is the best way to see it. At first, the city may seem as bewildering as the maze in *Alice's Adventures in Wonderland,* but it helps to remember that downtown is divided into four sections: northeast, northwest, southeast, and southwest, with the Capitol in the center. Streets are clearly marked, and the National Park Service has information booths dotting the downtown area. They'll gladly give you a map—and that's free, too!

First things first. Begin your explorations as Washington itself began, with the federal city.

THE FEDERAL CITY

▶ Wake up early to see the White House, for this is Washington's most popular tour. You'll visit the elegant East Room, where Abigail Adams's wash was hung, the Blue Room, with the portrait of President Washington that Dolley Madison saved from the fire, the grand Red and Green rooms, and the State Dining Room, too.

▶ Stop to rest on the Ellipse, the huge grassy oval behind the White House. Union soldiers camped here during the Civil War, but now it's a park where groups gather for everything from picnics to protests.

▶ Follow the footsteps of famous Americans to the Capitol. Walk through the ten-ton bronze doors that highlight events in the life of Christopher Columbus, and look up at scenes of American history painted on the ceiling of the Rotunda.

A. ▼   B. ▲   C. ▼

THIS PAGE: A. The huge oil paintings that circle the rotunda show events in American history. B. *M* stands for Metro and the entrance to Washington's subway system. C. Visitors touring the Federal Bureau of Investigation meet yesterday's fugitives face to face.

OPPOSITE PAGE: A. Postage stamps and food stamps, as well as money, are printed at the Bureau of Engraving and Printing. B. About forty million dollars in bills roll off the presses daily at the Bureau of Engraving and Printing. C. The Mall is great for kids and kites.

A. ▲ B. ▲ C. ▼

▶ Ask your senator or representative for permission to eat lunch in one of the Capitol restaurants. By order of Congress, bean soup is always on the menu.

▶ Read all about it in the Library of Congress. Look at a Stradivarius violin—or at the largest collection of comic books in the world!

▶ Climb the steps to the Supreme Court building. Gaze at the red-draped chamber and at the nine black-robed justices sitting at their long "bench." When the Court's not meeting, you can watch a film.

▶ Catch the shark feeding in the huge Commerce Department Building. Its basement is home to the National Aquarium, and to one thousand different kinds of fish.

▶ Put the Old Post Office on your list. You'll get an eagle's-eye view of the city from its 315-foot clock tower, second only to the Washington Monument in height.

▶ Duck into the J. Edgar Hoover FBI Building. The Federal Bureau of Investigation puts on a live firearm performance.

▶ Seeing is believing at the Bureau of Engraving and Printing. Watch hundreds of thousands of real dollars roll off the high-speed presses.

▶ Stop by the National Archives, storehouse of our nation's history. See the Declaration of Independence, the Constitution, and the Bill of Rights, or find your own family history in the research room.

THE MALL AND THE MUSEUMS

▶ Washington's Mall, designed by L'Enfant, is a tree-lined, two-mile strip of grass that stretches from Capitol Hill to the Lincoln Memorial. Along the route you can stop for a snack, ride the carousel, or visit any or all of the nine Smithsonian Museums on or near the Mall.

▶ Look to the sky at the National Air and Space Museum, the most visited museum in the world. Follow man's flights from the Wright brothers' first airplane to the *Apollo-Soyuz* international space mission.

▶ Go from tremendous to tiny at the National Museum of Natural History. See the full-sized model of a blue whale, the largest animal of all time, and then inspect honeybees in their hive at the Insect Zoo.

▶ Step back in time at the National Museum of American History. See Alexander Graham Bell's first telephone, Ford's Model T car, and the original flag that inspired "The Star-Spangled Banner."

▶ Marvel at working machines from a century past at the Arts and Industries Building. There's everything from an ice-cream maker to a gigantic steam locomotive.

▶ Treat yourself to some art. The West Building of the National Gallery of Art features traditional art; the East Building introduces modern art. A moving sidewalk on the lower level connects the two galleries, and an underground waterfall splashes beside it.

A., B., C. Everything's looking up at the National Air and Space Museum. D. Children take part in the exhibits at the Capital Children's Museum. E. A marble and metal garden grows at the Joseph H. Hirshhorn Sculpture Garden.

A. ▲

B. ▼ C. ▼

D. ▼ E. ▼

A. The Navy Memorial Museum has five thousand different things to look at. B. Visitors hunt for jungle creatures in Henri Rousseau's painting in the National Gallery of Art. C. Alexander Calder's mobile swings over the courtyard of the East Building of the National Gallery of Art.

A. ▲ B. ▲ C. ▼

▶ Find out what famous Americans from times past looked like at the National Portrait Gallery in the old Patent Office Building. Surround yourself with art from the present time at the Joseph H. Hirshhorn Museum and Sculpture Garden. Take a tour especially for children at the Arthur M. Sackler Gallery for Asian and Near Eastern art. Go underground to discover African culture at the National Museum of African Art. Most of this museum is built below street level.

Now leave the Mall to:

▶ Make your own Mexican tortilla, or crawl through a sewer pipe at the Capital Children's Museum.

▶ See toys that your great-great-great-great-great-grandparents might have played with in the Children's Attic at the Daughters of the American Revolution headquarters.

▶ Watch moving Lionel toy trains and see an old-fashioned schoolroom at the Dolls' House and Toy Museum of Washington.

▶ Climb onto a tank or peer through a periscope at the Washington Navy Yard and Navy Memorial Museum.

▶ Explore the National Geographic Society's Explorers Hall and be part of one hundred years of adventure around the world.

▶ Get acquainted with Washington's own African American heritage at the Smithsonian's Anacostia Museum. There's a place for picnics here, too.

▶ Don't leave the Anacostia community without visiting

the Frederick Douglass Home. The house of this famous black abolitionist is now a museum in his memory.

MONUMENTS AND MEMORIALS

▶ The whole city of Washington is a memorial to our first president. But you can't miss the Washington Monument rising at the west end of the Mall. Ride an elevator to the top of the obelisk and see the capital spread out below.

▶ Visit the Lincoln Memorial at night if you can. Lights illuminate the sad expression on Abraham Lincoln's face and gleam from the Reflecting Pool in front of the memorial.

▶ And don't forget to meet Thomas Jefferson in his memorial beside the Tidal Basin.

▶ Walk slowly past the Vietnam Veterans Memorial and read the names of those lost in the Vietnam conflict. The two black granite walls, shaped in a V, cast back the world around them like dark mirrors.

▶ Cross the Arlington Memorial Bridge over the Potomac River to Arlington National Cemetery. Watch the changing of the guard at the Tomb of the Unknowns and see the eternal flame flickering on the grave of President John F. Kennedy.

▶ Beside Arlington's entrance, notice the new memorial being built to honor women who served in the armed forces.

▶ Go on to the U.S. Marine Corps War Memorial. The statue captures a moment in 1945 when the American flag was raised on Iwo Jima, an island in the western Pacific.

AND MORE . . .

▶ Visit the John F. Kennedy Center for the Performing Arts. Inside are three theaters, an opera house, a concert hall, and a movie house. Outside, there's a great view over the Potomac River.

▶ Try your hand at brass rubbing at the National Cathedral. There's a children's chapel there, too.

▶ Step into other countries along Embassy Row. The Islamic Mosque and Cultural Center has a sky-piercing 160-foot minaret. Take off your shoes before you enter!

▶ Tour Ford's Theatre, or even attend a play. The theater has been restored to look as it did on the night that Abraham Lincoln was shot. Then cross the street to the Petersen House to view the small bed in which the president died.

▶ Join the sightseers at historic Union Station. More than a busy train terminal, it's the capital's tribute to the railroads.

THIS PAGE: A. The Vietnam Veterans Memorial names those who died in that conflict. B. The Tomb of the Unknowns at Arlington National Cemetery is watched over by an honor guard.

OPPOSITE PAGE: A. An Eternal Flame flickers on the grave of President John F. Kennedy in Arlington Cemetery. B. The Marine Corps War Memorial is also called the Iwo Jima Memorial.

A. ▼ B. ▼

▶ See the House of the Americas, headquarters of the Organization of American States. When you stand in its Aztec garden, you will be in the exact geographical center of Washington, D.C.

▶ Wander the brick sidewalks of Georgetown, Washington's oldest section. Jog along the towpath of the Chesapeake & Ohio (C&O) Canal.

▶ Spend a day in Rock Creek Park. It's Washington's wilderness with bike paths and fifteen miles of hiking trails. Within the park is the National Zoo. Greet Smokey the Bear and the Chinese pandas, and walk right into a world of birds—the Great Flight Cage!

▶ Dip into Washington's waters. Pedal a paddleboat on the Tidal Basin, take a mule-drawn barge ride on the C&O Canal, or cruise down the Potomac River to visit Mount Vernon, George Washington's plantation.

▶ Then . . . plan to come back to the capital to do all the things you missed!

A.▼   B.▼

A POCKETFUL
OF FACTS

Washington, D.C., has been the capital of the United States of America since the federal government moved to the city on December 1, 1800.

The city of Washington and the District of Columbia share the same boundaries, bordered on the north by the state of Maryland and on the south by the state of Virginia.

The area included is about sixty-nine square miles, but since both the Potomac and the Anacostia rivers flow through the city, six square miles of this area is under water. Another twelve square miles has been set aside as parkland. Two islands, both in the Potomac River, are included in the District's boundaries—Theodore Roosevelt Island and Columbia Island, also known as Lady Bird Johnson Park.

Washington has about 626,000 residents, making it sixteenth in population size among American cities. Over three and a half million people live in the greater Washington metropolitan area.

The highest point in Washington, where the television transmitters are located, is 410 feet above sea level, in the northwest section of the city.

Washington is governed differently from other cities in

the United States. In 1973, when Congress granted the District of Columbia a self-governing charter, citizens were given the right to elect their own mayor and thirteen-member city council. These officials are elected for four-year terms. The District can raise money through taxes, but Congress supervises the budget. Congress may also vote to overrule city decisions.

Since 1961, when the states approved the Twenty-third Amendment to the Constitution, citizens of the District of Columbia have been allowed to vote for president and vice-president of the United States. Since 1970, they have been able to elect a delegate to the House of Representatives. The delegate may serve on a committee, but, because the District of Columbia is not a state, this representative cannot vote on the floor.

SYMBOLS

District motto: *Justitia omnibus* (Justice for All)

District seal: Adopted in 1871, shows a woman representing Justice placing a wreath on a statue of George Washington

District flag: Two red stripes and three red stars on a white field. Adopted in 1938, it is based upon George Washington's family coat of arms.

District bird: Wood thrush

District tree: Scarlet oak

District flower: American beauty rose

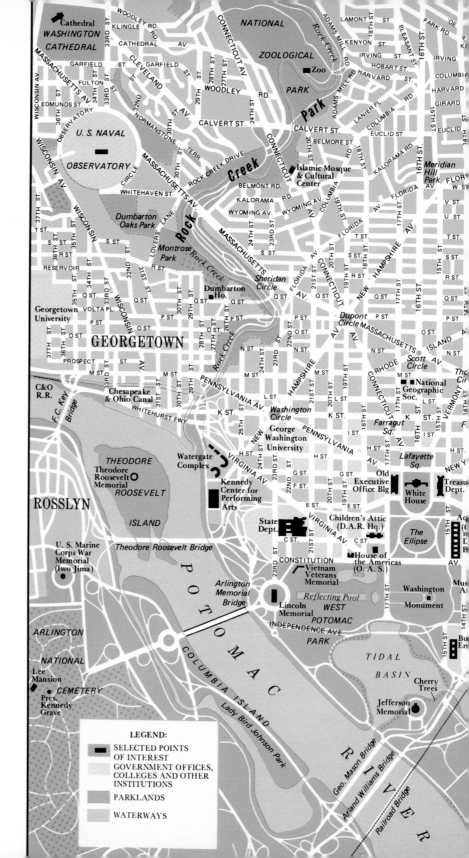

WOODLEY RD.
KLINGLE
CATHEDRAL
AV.

Cathedral
WASHINGTON
CATHEDRAL

33RD ST.
KLINGLE ST.

MASSACHUSETTS AV.
GARFIELD ST.
28TH ST.
27TH ST.
WOODLEY RD.

CLEVELAND
GARFIELD

32ND

29TH

ST. AV.

32ND AV.
CALVERT ST.

EDMUNDS ST.
FULTON ST.

36TH
WISCONSIN AV.

OBSERVATORY CIRCLE

NORMANSTONE TERR.

U. S. NAVAL

OBSERVATORY

WHITEHAVEN ST.

WISCONSIN

37TH ST.

WISCONSIN AV.

Dumbarton
Oaks Park

ROCK CREEK DRIVE

Rock Creek

Creek

BELMONT RD.

KALORAMA
WYOMING AV.

Montrose
Park

Rock Creek

36TH ST.
35TH ST.
R ST.
34TH ST.

RESERVOIR
Q ST.

31ST ST.

30TH
Rock Creek

Georgetown
University
VOLTA PL.

P ST.
WISCONSIN

O ST.
O ST.

GEORGETOWN

37TH
36TH
PROSPECT
M ST.

35TH
34TH
33RD
ST.

WISCONSIN AV.

30TH
31ST
M ST.

29TH
M ST.

C&O
R.R.

F.C. Key Bridge

Chesapeake
& Ohio Canal

31ST ST.

WHITEHURST FWY.
K ST.

NATIONAL

ZOOLOGICAL

Zoo

PARK

Park

CALVERT ST.

ADAMS MILL RD.
KENYON
ST.

LAMONT ST.

IRVING ST.

HOBART ST.

HARVARD

COLUMBIA
RD.

BELMORE ST.

20TH ST.

LANIER PL.

EUCLID ST.

18TH ST.

19TH ST.

Islamic Mosque
& Cultural
Center

Meridian
Hill
Park

FLOR
W ST.

V ST.

U ST.

KALORAMA RD.

BELMONT RD.

KALORAMA
RD.

WYOMING AV.

COLUMBIA AV.

FLORIDA AV.

NEW HAMPSHIRE

16TH ST.

17TH ST.

T ST.

S ST.

R ST.

Sheridan
Circle

FLORIDA

24TH ST.

23RD ST.

FLORIDA AV.

CONNECTICUT AV.

18TH ST.

19TH ST.

Q ST.

Dumbarton
Ho.

28TH
27TH
P ST.

26TH
P ST.

25TH
N ST.

23RD

22ND

Q ST.

O ST.

N ST.

P ST.

MASSACHUSETTS

HAMPSHIRE

20TH
21ST

19TH ST.

Dupont
Circle MASSACHUSETTS

NEW

ISLAND

A

RHODE

CONNECTICUT AV.

Scott
Circle

The
Cir

VERMONT

PENNSYLVANIA AV.

Washington
Circle

George
Washington
University

24TH

23RD

M ST.
L ST.

21ST ST.
20TH ST.

M ST.
L ST.

National
Geographic
Soc.

L ST.

K ST.

Farragut
Sq.

17TH ST.

16TH

15TH ST.

14TH

VIRGINIA AV.

Watergate
Complex

Kennedy
Center for
Performing
Arts

NEW
VIRGINIA AV.

25TH

24TH
23RD

H ST.
G ST.
F ST.

22ND

E ST.

PENNSYLVANIA

22ND ST.

21ST ST.
20TH ST.

19TH ST.

H ST.

G ST.
F ST.

E ST.

Lafayette
Sq.

Old
Executive
Office Blg

White
House

NEW Y

Treasu
Dept.

THEODORE
ROOSEVELT

Theodore
Roosevelt
Memorial

ROOSEVELT

ROSSLYN

ISLAND

State
Dept.

VIRGINIA AV.

Children's Attic
(D.A.R. Hq.)

C ST.

The
Ellipse

Aq
(C
N
L B

U. S. Marine
Corps War
Memorial
(Iwo Jima)

Theodore Roosevelt Bridge

23RD ST.

CONSTITUTION

House of
the Americas
(O. A. S.)

17TH ST.

AV.

15TH ST.

ARLINGTON

P
O
T
O
M
A
C

Arlington
Memorial
Bridge

Vietnam
Veterans
Memorial

Reflecting Pool

Lincoln
Memorial

WEST

POTOMAC

INDEPENDENCE AVE.

PARK

Washington
Monument

14TH ST.

Mus
A

NATIONAL

Lee
Mansion

CEMETERY
Pres.
Kennedy
Grave

COLUMBIA ISLAND

Lady Bird Johnson Park

Geo. Mason Bridge

Arland Williams Bridge

Railroad Bridge

TIDAL

BASIN

Cherry
Trees

Jefferson
Memorial

15TH ST.

Bu
En

R
I
V
E
R

LEGEND:

SELECTED POINTS
OF INTEREST
GOVERNMENT OFFICES,
COLLEGES AND OTHER
INSTITUTIONS

PARKLANDS

WATERWAYS

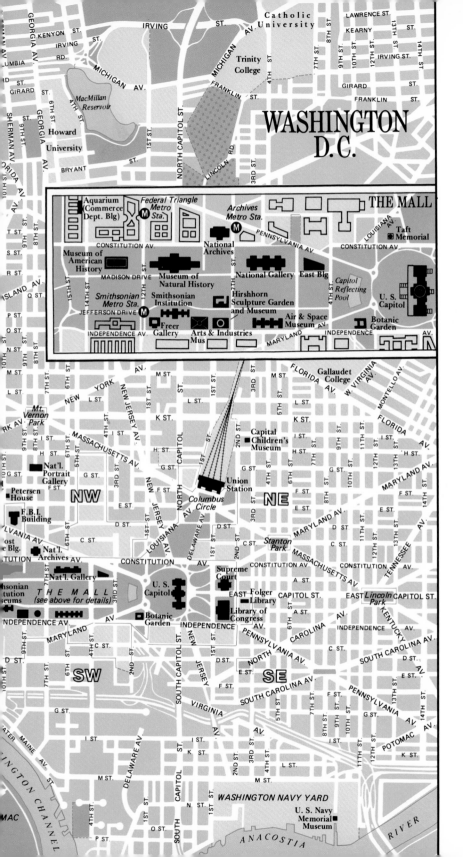

INDEX

A. The National Cathedral serves all denominations. B. Amtrak trains come and go at grand old Union Station. C. A mule on the tow path pulls a barge along the C&O Canal. D. In front of the Jefferson Memorial, small boats navigate the Tidal Basin's choppy waters.

A.▲　B.▲

C.▲　D.▼